The Great Trash Bash

The Great Trash Bash

LOREEN LEEDY

SCHOLASTIC INC.
New York   Toronto   London   Auckland   Sydney

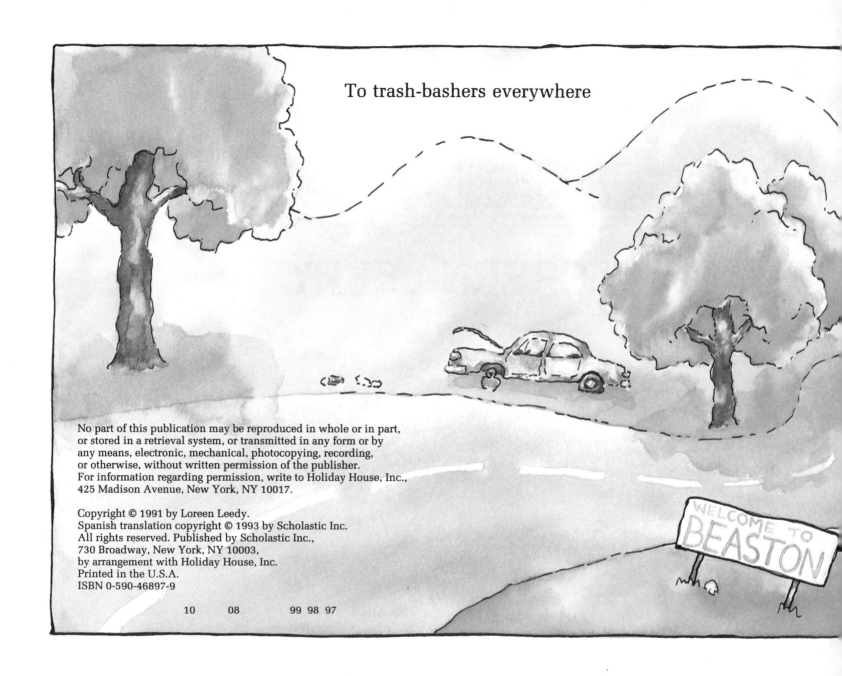

To trash-bashers everywhere

Copyright © 1991 by Loreen Leedy.
Spanish translation copyright © 1993 by Scholastic Inc.
All rights reserved. Published by Scholastic Inc.,
730 Broadway, New York, NY 10003,
by arrangement with Holiday House, Inc.
Printed in the U.S.A.
ISBN 0-590-46897-9

10   08   99 98 97

WELCOME TO BEASTON

There are rolling hills and wiggly roads and shady trees in Beaston. It is a home to any animal that can run, fly or swim. But something is wrong.

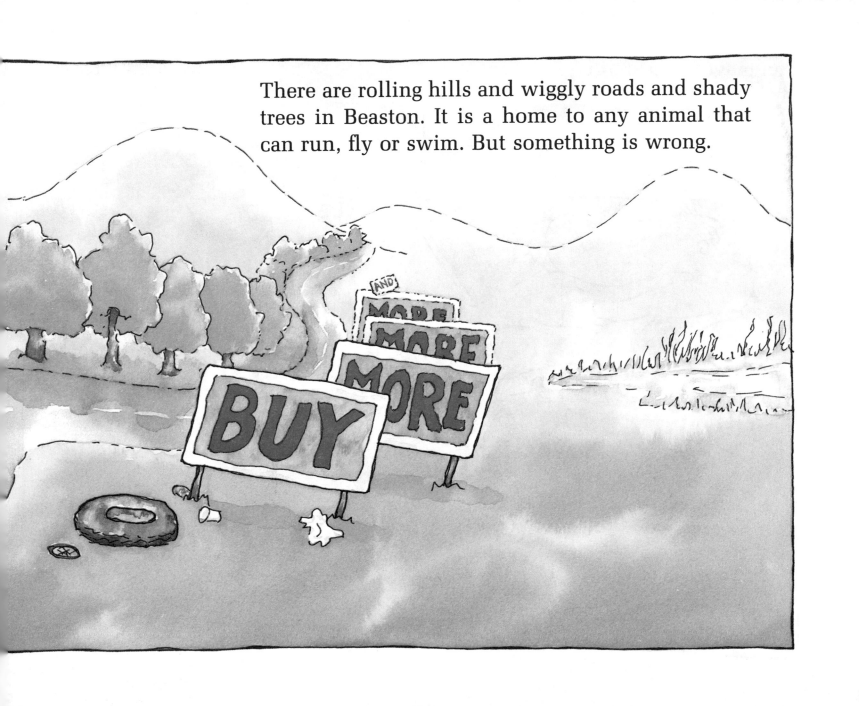

The mayor is searching for an answer.

He talks to citizens wherever he goes.

At last, Mayor Hippo finds the answer.

To find out more about trash, the mayor goes to the dump.

Next, he visits the incinerator.

The landfill is the last stop.

Mayor Hippo calls a town meeting.

At the meeting, the animals think of ways to solve the trash problem. They start to make changes in their everyday life.

Citizens take out their tools.

They start to clean up Beaston.

They even find some good uses for trash.

Soon, the town opens a recycling center.

In the recycling center, the trash is sorted out.

There are rolling hills and wiggly roads and shady trees in Beaston. It is a home to any animal that can run, fly or swim. Beaston is a beautiful place.

HERE ARE SOME IDEAS FOR CUTTING DOWN ON TRASH:

1. Use dishes instead of disposable cups and plates.
2. Keep junk mail for scrap paper.
3. Buy products made from recycled materials.
4. Avoid buying products with several layers of packaging.
5. Repair broken items instead of buying new ones.
6. Buy beverages in returnable bottles.
7. Reuse a large envelope by attaching a new address label.
8. Save glass, metal, paper, cartons, and plastic to recycle.
9. Pick up litter on roadsides.
10. Encourage parents to use cloth diapers—(disposable diapers fill up landfills).
11. Donate extra clothes and toys to charity.
12. Buy new products only if you really need them.
13. Don't waste paper. Write on both sides.